MW01611112

A Dog to Remember

By June Greig

Illustrations by Gina Duffy

ISBN: 978-0-615-44339-3
Evergreen Bay Publishing
www.adogtoremember.com

to Bailey

in gratitude for a great love shared

"When we have the deepest of affection for a dog, we do not possess that love but are possessed by it, and sometimes it takes us by surprise, overwhelms us."

Dean Koontz, "A Big Little Life"

In memory of

Tessa

You are my star

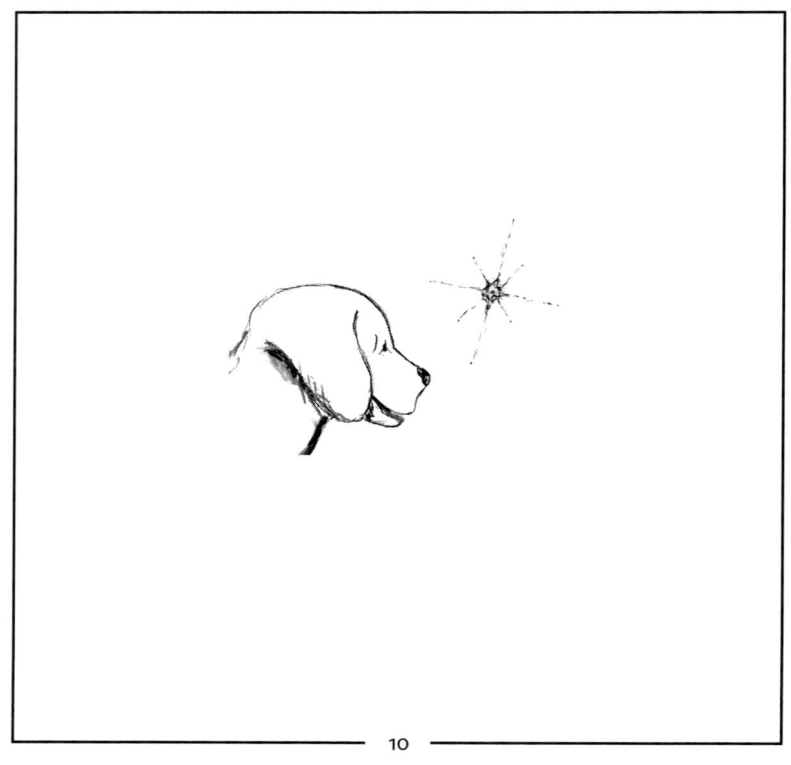

Forever to shine

Sweet memories
of you

Stay on my mind.

You still bring
me warmth

Though I miss your soft touch

You still make me smile

Though I miss you so much

I think of our walks

And our simple talks

I remember your loyal,
trusting ways.

All the joy and the laughs,

And the comfort we shared,

You were at my side every day.

We may be apart

But not in my heart

Sweet memories of you

Stay in my thoughts.

I still see those eyes

That had so much to say

I still feel your love,

Though you're so far away.